Remembering Obama's Mob Rule

Through Illustrations

About the Cover

Obama is turning his back on America and at the same time killing the structure that made this country great, the U.S. Constitution and Capitalism.

Remembering Obama's Mob Rule

Through Illustrations

Written and Illustrated
by George V. Rikard

Acknowledgments

Thanks to Mrs. Libia Chapman for her support, understanding and patience.

Thanks also to my daughter, Mrs. Victoria Conley, for her support and hours of painstaking editorial assistance.

I would like to thank Steve Rikard, my son for his support and advice.

ISBN: 145154295X

EAN-13: 9781451542950

Printed in the United States of America.

Contents

Introduction

The purpose of this book is to remind you what Obama and his Chicago-style political team have done to the country and what the damage will be if he and his congressional supporters are re-elected to a second term.

You'll see President Elect Obama's dissention from Mt. Chicago with ghosts of "Al Capone" and the "St. Valentines Day Massacre" left behind.

Without support from the Mainstream Media and Organized Labor Obama goes nowhere. Only with their help does Obama reach the White House. To get Obama a second term, he will need to change direction in his course to "Fundamentally transform the United States of America," but Obama is too deeply committed to his vision of himself as the savior of the Free World, and most likely will continue on his progressive course, which is opposite to what the country needs or wants.

You'll be reminded of several campaign promises Obama made. The question is did he keep them? If you believe Obama did not keep his promises, can you believe his rhetoric today?

Progressive individuals will be addressed from time to time. Progressives think they are the only ones smart enough to make decisions for the country. The common folk don't know how to make decisions, so the Progressives will make laws that suit them. Never mind what the country wants. The Progressives create a problem, and then come up with a solution. Remember when Obama said that GM and Chrysler were too big to fail and if we don't help them, millions of jobs will be lost. How many jobs have been lost since he said that? What Obama didn't say was he was actually paying the auto unions back for their support during his Presidential campaign. At the same time he was taking control of a part of the economy. Similar techniques were used for banks, insurance and the housing bubble. Now the government has control over a large part of the economy and that, dear friend, is the aim of the progressive movement. They want to control the United States of America. This is what Obama meant when he said "We are five days away from Fundamentally Transforming the United States of America." John McCain's daughter calls herself a "Progressive Republican" and Hillary Clinton calls herself a "Modern Progressive." No matter how they word it, a progressive is still a progressive. They want to remake our society according to their radical views, which means they will control everything. The progressives also believe the constitution is a living document that should change as the country changes. Can you imagine Obama changing our rights to suite him? That's exactly what Obama is doing.

You'll find the story line is carried out by illustrations with some commentary to enhance, high-light or help explain a given situation. All these represent my opinions that were formed by my thoughts, feelings and impressions of the situations as they occurred.

Along with the actual events, my opinions could not have been complete without a few reading assignments "American Progressivism" edited by Ronald J. Pestritto and William J. Atto, "Rules for Radicals" by Saul D. Alinsky, "Arguing with Idiots" by Glen Beck, and "Barack Obama's Rules for Revolution, the Alinsky Model" by David Horowitz. Listening to TV opinion from Liberals and Conservatives gave me the information to illustrate the following situations. You may or may not agree with me, That's fine.

You'll find note pages for thoughts you have as you go through the book. You can use them for review before you vote in November.

"Beware of false prophets who come to you in sheep's clothing but inwardly are ravenous wolves. You will know them by their fruits."

Matthew 7:15 (Revised
Standard Version)

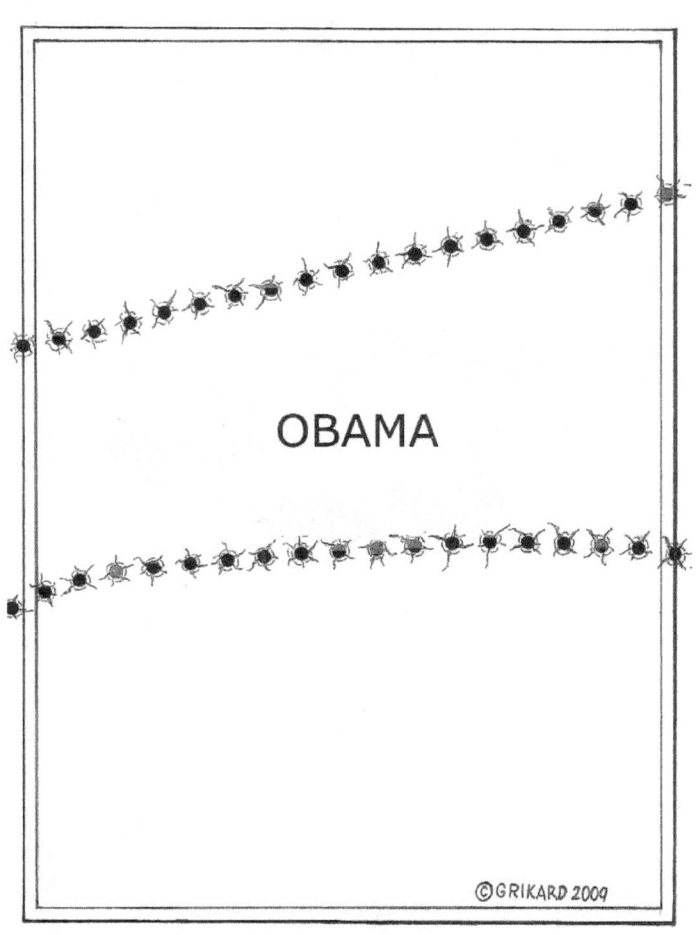

Only Obama supporters are allowed
to vote here!

Campaign Promises

President Obama's campaign promises are as empty as his rhetoric about Gitmo, Health care, Stimulus, Omnibus and giving terrorists' citizenship rights.

14

Let's compare some of Obama's campaign promises to what has actually taken place. According to Obama, Gitmo must be closed because the terrorists use it as a recruiting tool. Al Qaeda didn't need a recruiting tool to attack us on 9/11. Do you really think they need one now?

According to Obama, Health Care Reform will lower premiums, the deficit, and cover the uninsured. Wrong. The dealings made behind closed doors such as Cadillac Health Care Taxes, special financial favors to supporters, states and special interest groups have poisoned the public against the bill. Obama's compromise technique is to ask non-supporters how much they want to support his program. The corruption will require fewer states to carry a larger Health Care financial burden which will be passed on to the consumer in the form of increased premiums. One way Obama lowered the Health Care cost was not include the doctors' closed door deal in the bill. I guess Obama thinks doctors are not part of the Health Care System. Another method Obama is using to make the Health Care Bill look like it is reducing the deficit is known as the 10-4 accounting scam. You and I, the consumer, will pay for Health Care Reform the entire ten years, but only receive major benefits the last four years. Anybody else using the same accounting system will be in prison. We must elect representatives that will follow the constitution.

Something tells me Obama's Health Care Reform Bill will not cover everyone. Some people say they are healthy and don't want the coverage. Others have enough money and don't need the insurance and some are illegal immigrants that according to Federal Law shouldn't have the insurance.

Remember Obama saying "If we pass the $787 billion dollar Stimulus Bill, unemployment will not exceed 8%." Where's the unemployment now? The only thing stimulated was Obama supporters. And, who can forget Obama speaking before a joint session of Congress declaring how the $410 billion dollar Omnibus bill was better than peanut butter, but forgot to mention the 8,500 earmarks. He probably had peanut butter stuck on the roof of his mouth and couldn't spit it out.

Here's another Obama decision. He and his Attorney General will be giving Constitutional Rights to terrorists and possibly bring them to the states for prosecution. I can hear Bin Laden now, "don't worry if you get captured, the stupid infidels will give you a lawyer, who will advise you of your rights." Talk about a recruiting tool.

Leave the Black Panthers alone.
They helped to elect me.

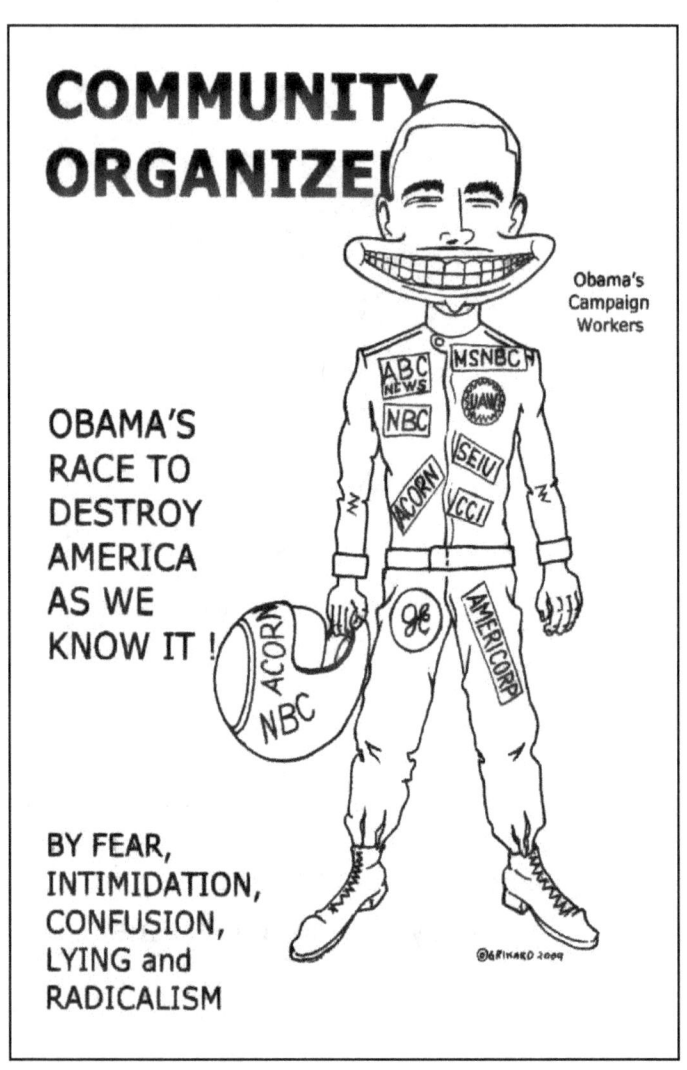

President Obama

President Obama will be remembered as the first and hopefully the only president to be elected by the Mainstream Media (MSM). When the MSM reports positive news about a candidate and refuses to report negative news, an injustice is perpetrated on the public. The result is a President being elected by one source. That sounds like Communism to me, or is it Progressivism?

Obama was never vetted and as of this writing, the citizens of the United States still do not know about Obama, the Community Organizer. We are slowly finding out what he stands for, and the more we find out, the more we dislike his agenda, political programs and his radical advisors. But what can you expect when you consider Obama's dance through Chicago's corrupt political system and his radical associates, such as Bill Ayres, Reverent Wright and gangster style Czars.

Since Obama became President, Czars claim to be communist and some openly claim that Mao is someone to be looked up to. What kind of government do we have? The question should be what kind of government do we want? Would you vote for Obama again knowing what kind of advisors he has around? I believe Obama is as corrupt as the system he came out of and is as crooked as the Rocky Mountains. I wouldn't trust him with your dime, much less mine.

In conclusion, a man becomes the organizations and associates in which he dwells.

The unions will control the U.S. Financial system!

Obama Descending from Mt. Chicago

Here we have Obama descending from Mt. Chicago on his way to Washington D.C. with the persuasive techniques he will use to govern. You will see Obama use fear and speed to push his progressive bills through Congress, so the public and opposition can't read the bills. How can you defeat a bill if you don't know what's in it? Obama will use threats, lies, deception, intimidation, confusion and money to get support for his progressive programs.

The bills and programs will be introduced with statements like, we need this bill to level the playing field, or a group of people or company is to big to fail. You will also hear, it's for the good of the country/environment. Don't believe them. The only thing Progressives want is to control every aspect of our lives. They don't think the general public is smart enough to do things on their own, so the Progressive intellects will do the thinking and make the decisions.

Mr. President, I'm in charge here. You'll do as I say or I'll send you back to Chicago. Do you understand?
YES, MADAM SPEAKER.

I'll provide your speeches. Do your thing. CAMPAIGN! Do I make myself clear?

YES, MADAM SPEAKER.

You're excused.

President Elect Obama meets Nancy Pelosi

The inspiration to create the meeting goes back to a joint session of Congress where Obama proclaims his $410 billion Omnibus bill, the greatest thing since his birth. My attention centers on Pelosi jumping up and clapping with great enthusiasm as Obama is speaking. In fact, I thought she was too enthusiastic. Her actions caused me to question, why? The more I watched, the more I became intrigued. My thoughts centered on one word, ownership. I bet she wrote Obama's speech. After all, he hadn't done anything except run for office. Put another way, the only thing Obama has done is campaign and he's still doing it.

While I was watching Pelosi, I noticed that every time she jumped up, a half second later Biden would follow. I started laughing, because I put myself in Biden's place. If it was me, I would be looking for hammer and nails to nail her tail to the chair and the chair to the floor.

Chicago tactics

28

29

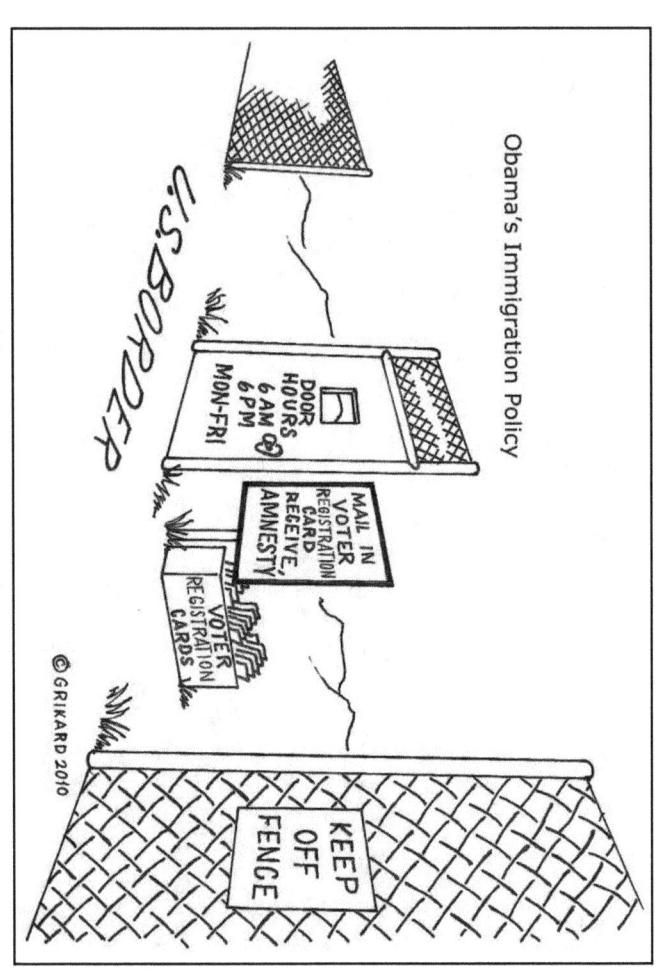

30

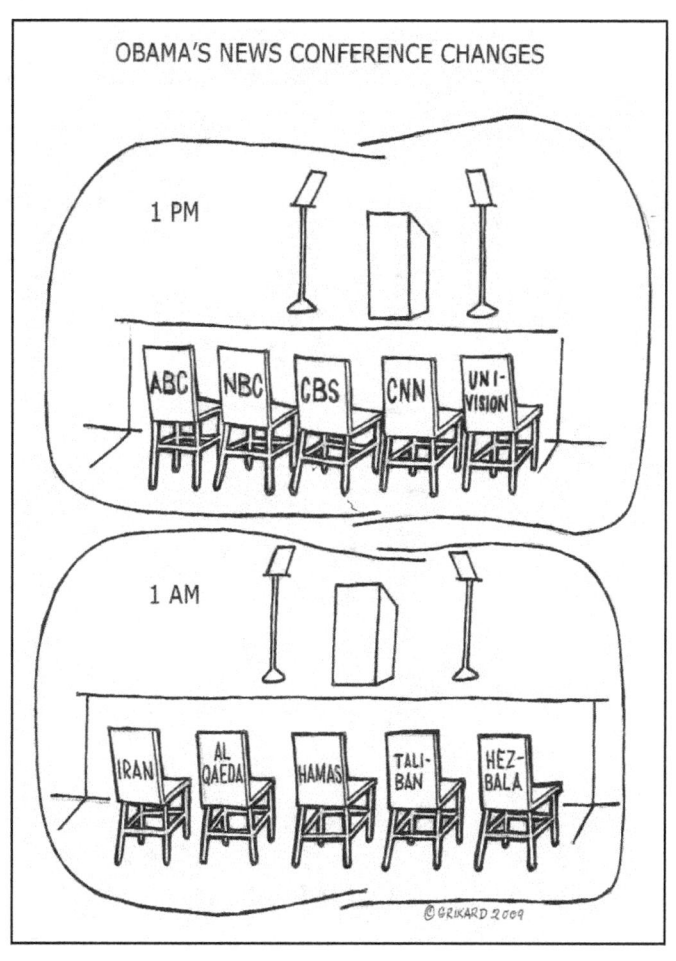

33

HEAR NO CAPITOLISM
SEE NO CAPITOLISM
SPEAK NO CAPITOLISM

Notes

_____

_____

_____

_____

_____

_____

_____

_____

_____

_____

_____

_____

_____

_____

_____

_____

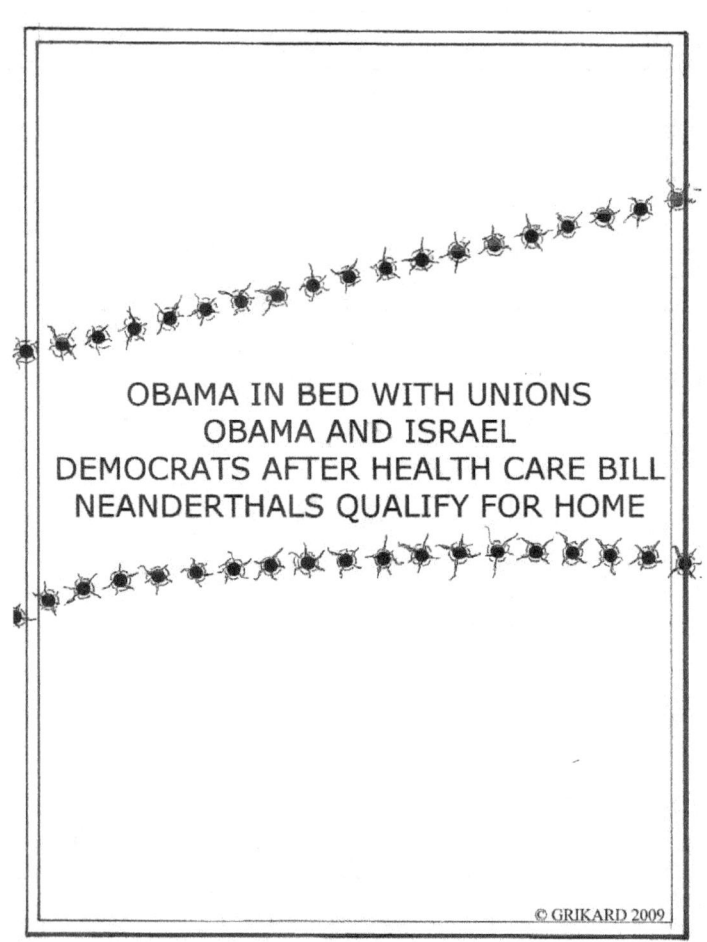

OBAMA IN BED WITH UNIONS
OBAMA AND ISRAEL
DEMOCRATS AFTER HEALTH CARE BILL
NEANDERTHALS QUALIFY FOR HOME

© GRIKARD 2009

38

39

41

Even Neanderthals can Qualify

Notes

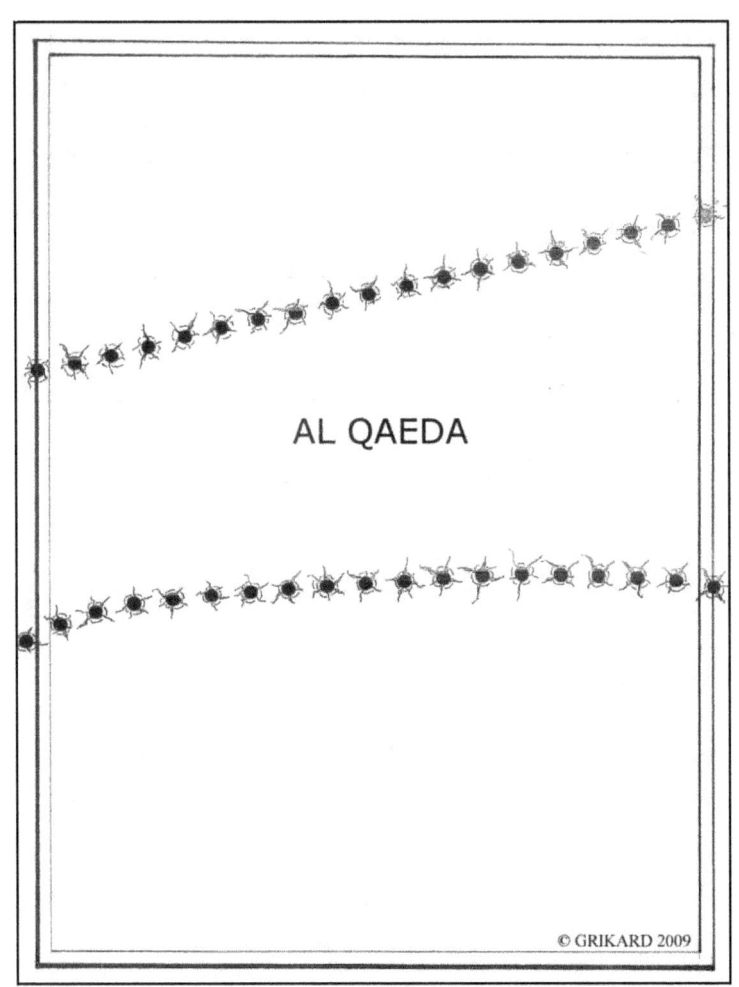

AL QAEDA

© GRIKARD 2009

I was slow responding to
the oil spill.

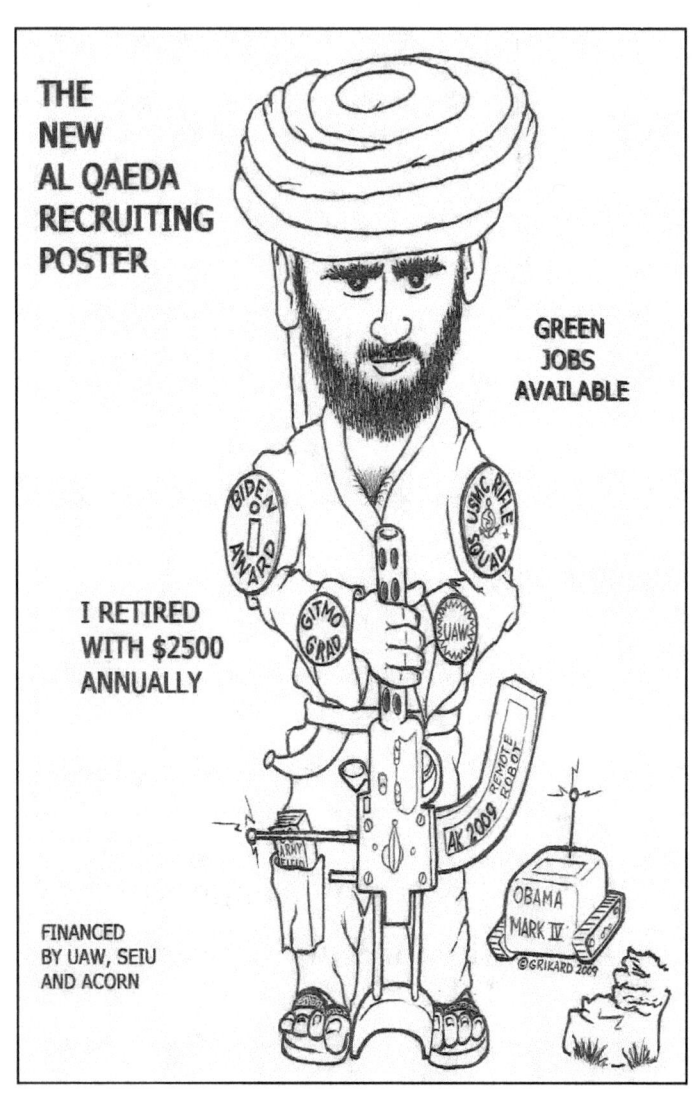

46

Al Qaeda

The way President Obama feels about terrorists is dangerous to say the least. Obama wants to "spread the wealth" to them as he does to the rest of the world. He wants to give the terrorists American Justice with all the Constitutional rights a common crook would receive. To level the field or spread the wealth sound like "Progressivism" to me. How about you? Bigger government is needed to divide the loot. Congress will make the decisions for you and I. They think they are the only ones capable of such matters.

Imagine if Al Qaeda worked with the Progressives? The terrorists over time would be able to retire with an annual annuity. Remember Obama wants to level the field. Al Qaeda would first need to take an oath to be good. They could then train with the US Marine Corp, receive a diploma from Gitmo, use the advanced infantry rifle, OBAMA (Overseas Battlefield Automatic Matrix Array), compete for shooting awards and possibly retire or get a green job in the states. Sound ridiculous? Yes. But the question remains. Is it possible?

GUANTANAMO BAY UNIVERSITY

Chartered in 2001
by the United States of America

By the Authority of the United States of America vested in the
Board of Trustees of Guantanamo Bay University and
upon recommendation of the Faculty thereof the degree of

Associate of Confinement
is conferred upon

The Sixth day of February in the year of our Lord
Two thousand and nine.

_____   _____
Guantanamo Czar   Homeland security

©GRIKARD 2009

48

Guantanamo Bay Diploma

The Obama Administration has given US Constitutional rights to terrorists. Would a diploma from Guantanamo be his next blundering decision? Remember, Obama has said he wants to "spread the wealth." What is Obama's definition of wealth? We know for sure his definition includes monetary, constitutional rights, organized labor and education for citizens. But the question remains. Are Gitmo terrorists included in Obama's definition to "spread the wealth"?

Al Qaeda Training

Al Qaeda Training

Can you imagine Al Qaeda training with the US Marine Corp? I can't either, but the way the Obama Administration is treating terrorists, nothing is out of the question! In my view, the only way this could happen is Obama starts paying Al Qaeda not to fight us, and at the same time give them access to the training if they take an oath to be good, switch sides and fight the other terrorists.

Do you think this is possible? Now that would be acting stupidly! Right?

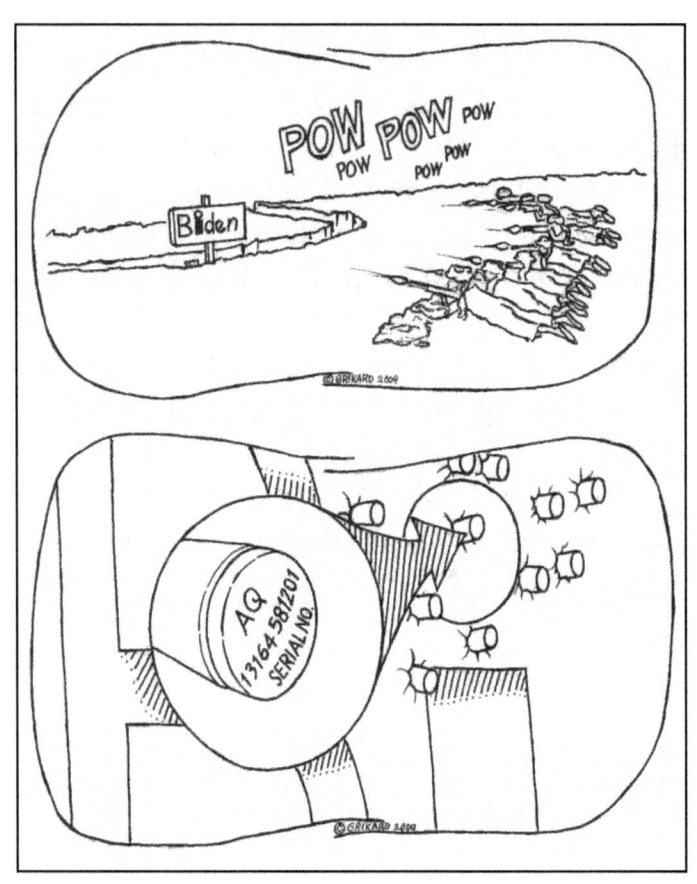

Al Qaeda Competition Shooting

Releasing terrorists from Gitmo is like saying, we don't think you received enough combat experience so, have another shot at it. Another way to say it is twenty per cent of the released terrorists return to the fight so go ahead and put a gun in their hands one more time.

Can you name a leader of any country in world history that has released suspected enemy troops while you are still at war with them?

The competition shooting will give the newly released terrorists some target practice before returning to the fight.

Some released terrorists do not return to the fight. They instead become leaders and train their terrorist comrades.

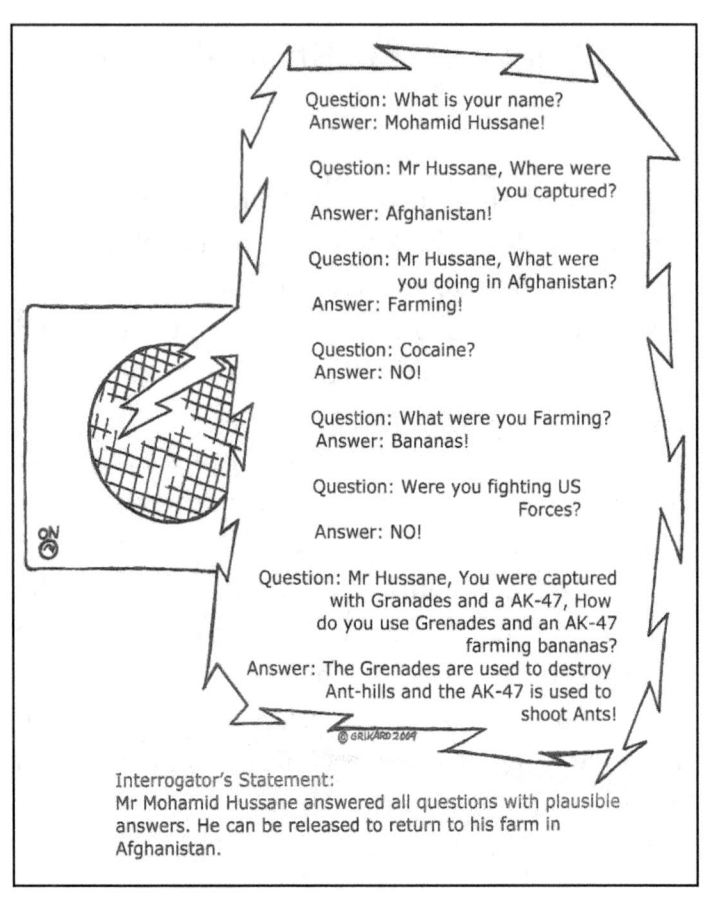

Question: What is your name?
Answer: Mohamid Hussane!

Question: Mr Hussane, Where were you captured?
Answer: Afghanistan!

Question: Mr Hussane, What were you doing in Afghanistan?
Answer: Farming!

Question: Cocaine?
Answer: NO!

Question: What were you Farming?
Answer: Bananas!

Question: Were you fighting US Forces?
Answer: NO!

Question: Mr Hussane, You were captured with Granades and a AK-47, How do you use Grenades and an AK-47 farming bananas?
Answer: The Grenades are used to destroy Ant-hills and the AK-47 is used to shoot Ants!

© GRIKARD 2009

Interrogator's Statement:
Mr Mohamid Hussane answered all questions with plausible answers. He can be released to return to his farm in Afghanistan.

54

White House Interrogation

Here we have a White House controlled interrogation taking place. While the interrogation is fictitious, how many interrogations has the White House performed?

When you consider how the President has treated terrorists, the interrogation is not that outrageous. The underwear bomber is another good example.

What do you think about the situation?

TRUTH, JUSTICE, the
AMERICAN WAY

© GRIKARD 2009

56

Truth and Justice the American Way

President Obama doesn't know the word truth and what it means. He will say one thing to get your support, then, do the opposite. Remember when he said earmarks will not be tolerated, or the Health Care Debate would be seen on C-SPAN. Has either of these promises been kept? No? In fact earmarks have actually increased and the Health Care Debate, if any took place, was behind closed doors.

The word justice means one thing to Obama if you support him, but something else if you don't. Remember the two black panthers outside a voting station where one was carrying a night stick? It has been reported the Justice Department dropped the charges after directions from the Attorney General's office. ACORN is another example of Obama's justice. Nothing up to this point and time has been done to put the guilty in jail. Also, the unions are exempt from paying the Health Care Cadillac taxes, while the remainder of the country will pay. Remember it's only until 2018. By then, Andy Sterns and SEIU will have made the exemption permanent.

Obama doesn't care about the American way of doing business. In my view, the free capitalist market is the only way the country will recover. If spending our way to prosperity worked, everyone with a large credit card balance will be a millionaire. The President only needs to look at California to see what will happen to the country if he continues with his spending spree. Obama wants to continue with his "spread the wealth" doctrine no matter the consequences. The very people Obama claims to help will be hurt the most. There's an old law called the "Gravitational law of Floods," which states, the low areas get water first. Put another way, the low income families will get hit with disaster after Obama spends all the people's money, China stops buying our debt and inflation raises its ugly head. These people depend on the government for their existence. If hyperinflation gets going, they will be wiped out, with no place to go. Remember fuel and food is not included in cost of living adjustments. Then you haven't seen anything yet! A look at Haiti will give you an idea of what could happen.

Phrases from the Obamas

During Mike Huckabee's interview with Michelle she uses the following phrase,
"You want to **create** the kind of country to pass on to your kids and grand-kids".
When Obama is elected President, Michelle says, "For the first time in my life, I'm proud of my country".

Obama says we need to:
 "Spread the wealth",
"It's good for the country",
"We are five days away from fundamentally transforming the United States of America",
"If we pass the $787 billion dollar Stimulus Bill, unemployment will not exceed 8%",
"Health Care Reform will lower premiums, the deficit, and cover the uninsured" ,
"Debate will be seen on C-Span",
"I will veto bills with Earmarks",
"No taxes, not one dime to the middle class, those making less than $250,000",
"My door is always open".

Progressivism in Government

One of the basic policies of progressivism is the government is the only entity capable of solving problems for the country. The common collective of the country doesn't have the smarts to solve national problems. Case in point, Obama decided it was morally right to give Health Care to 30 million individuals that don't have it, but to pay for those individual's Health Care, everyone in the country MUST buy Health Care or pay a fine. Never mind that the individuals who don't buy Health Care insurance don't want it for one reason or another. Obama says BUY it or else! What Obama isn't telling you is that illegal immigrants will reap the benefits of free Health Care after they are given amnesty. The result will be more democrats to keep Obama in office.

We as a country want LEGAL immigrants, but not immigrants that sneak through the back door. Are we a country of LAWS or a country of MAYBE laws when it suits you?

One more example. Obama wants the American criminal process distributed to terrorists, but according to the rules of war, don't deserve the process.

Notes

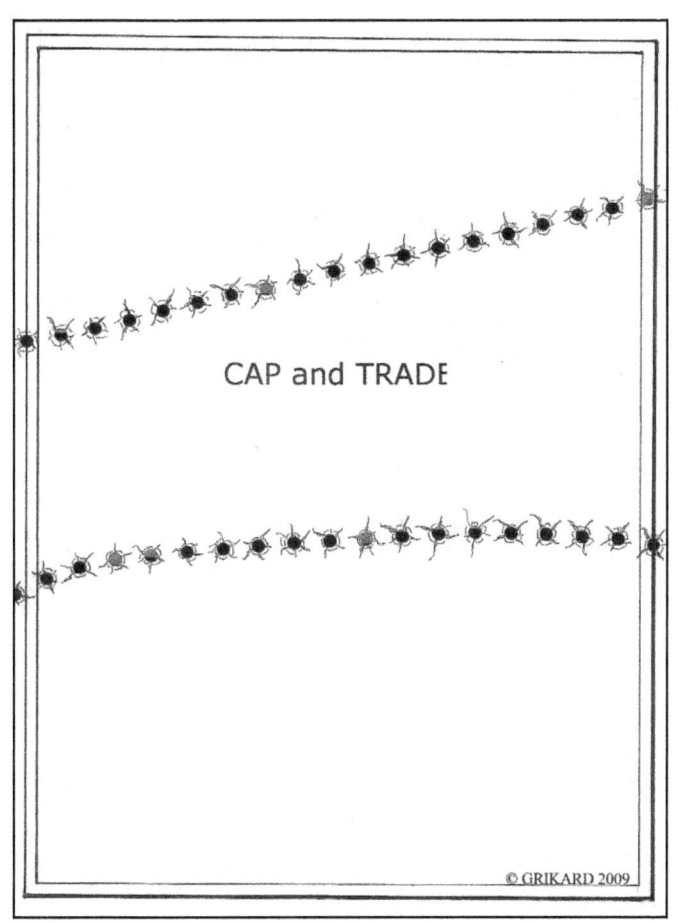

CAP and TRADE

© GRIKARD 2009

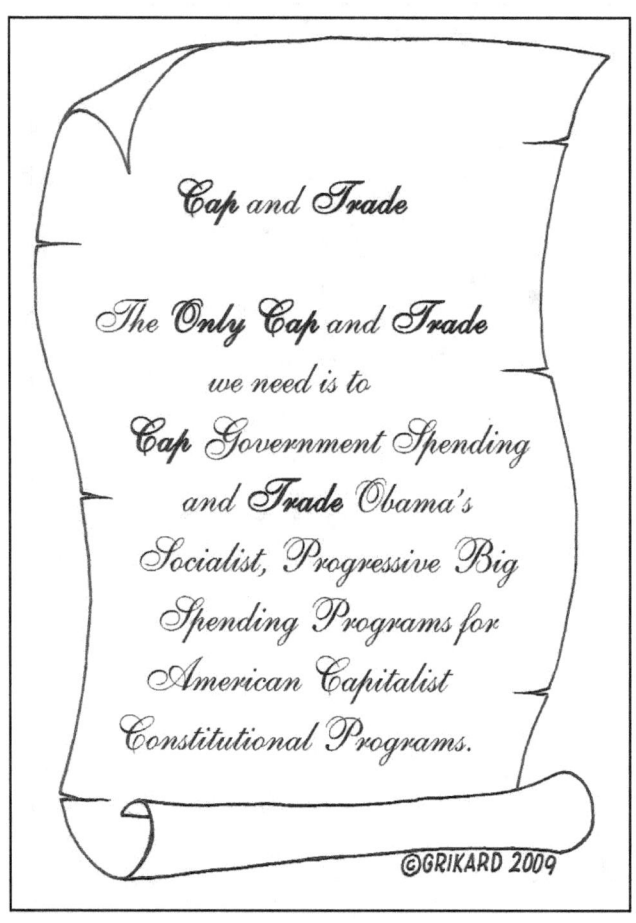

Cap and Trade

The Only Cap and Trade
we need is to
Cap Government Spending
and Trade Obama's
Socialist, Progressive Big
Spending Programs for
American Capitalist
Constitutional Programs.

©GRIKARD 2009

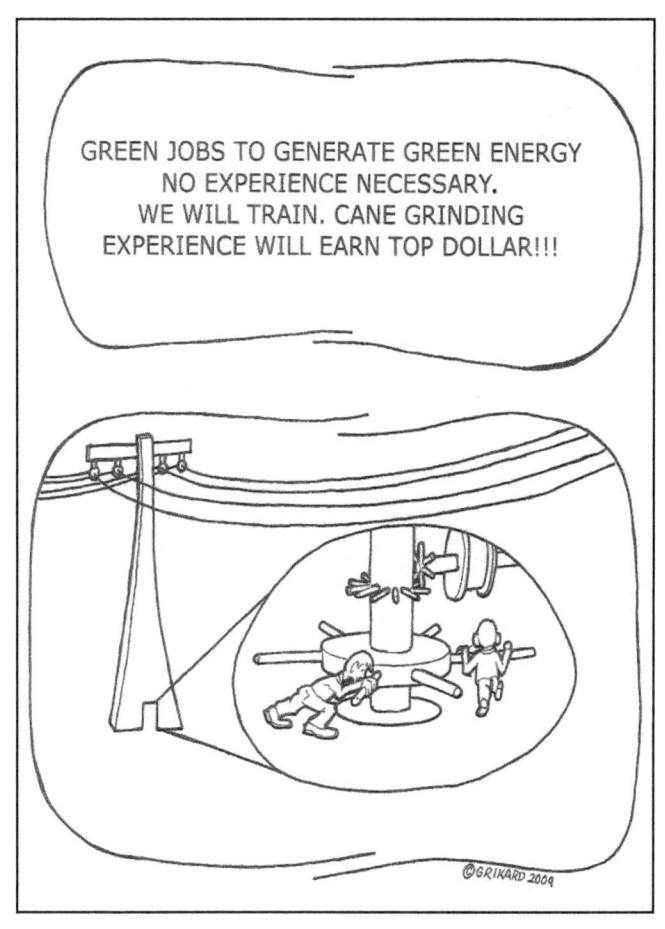

TEA PARTIES & FRIENDS
SHOVEL READY JOB
THE RIGHT WORD

© GRIKARD 2009

66

I will spend your tax dollars on my redistribution programs.

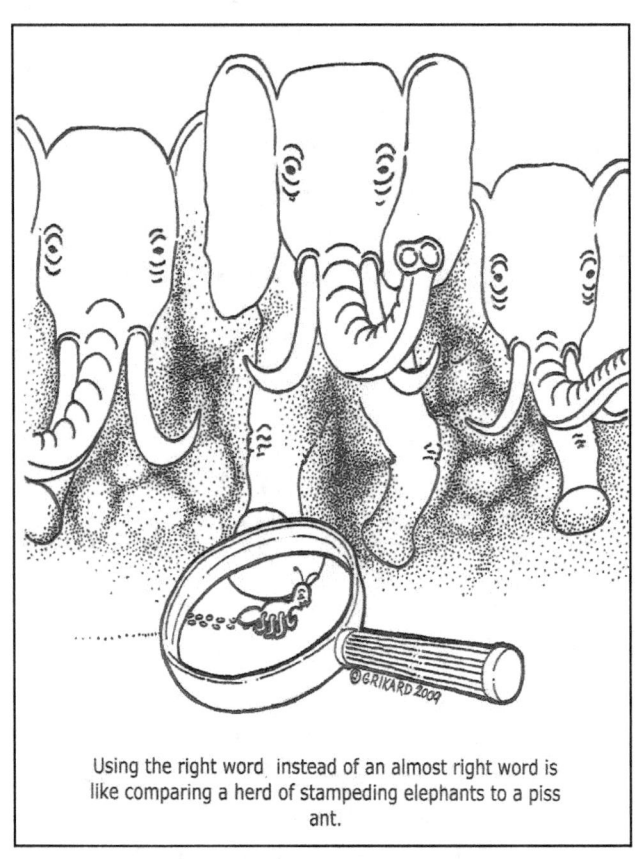

Using the right word, instead of an almost right word is like comparing a herd of stampeding elephants to a piss ant.

The Right Phrase or Word

The person who uses the right phrase or word controls the situation.

During Obama's Presidential Campaign he used the right remarks. Example: "change you can count on," "hope and change" "transform America" and "I will do everything in my power to make sure Iran doesn't get nuclear weapons." These are the words the public wanted to hear at that time.

After a year, Obama is now using the wrong phrases. Example: He's afraid to call a terrorist a "terrorist." He uses phrases like "man caused disaster" and "isolated extremist." Obama refuses to treat the terrorist that planned 9/11 as a terrorist, but instead will treat him as a common criminal. Giving him Constitutional rights and putting him on trial in America. Another example is the underwear bomber who was given Constitutional rights following 50 minutes of questioning. Talk about Al Qaeda recruiting information. The public doesn't want to hear Obama's weak- kneed phrases.

Both political parties use the same word *reform* to describe improvement to our health care system. If you listen to liberals, reform

71

means to scrap our existing system, and rebuild with the liberal plan. On the other hand, if you listen to conservatives, reform means to keep our existing system, and make adjustments to improve the system. When both parties use the same word, reform, confusion follows. There must be a difference between the parties before the public can make a choice. That's one reason the conservatives lost in 2008.

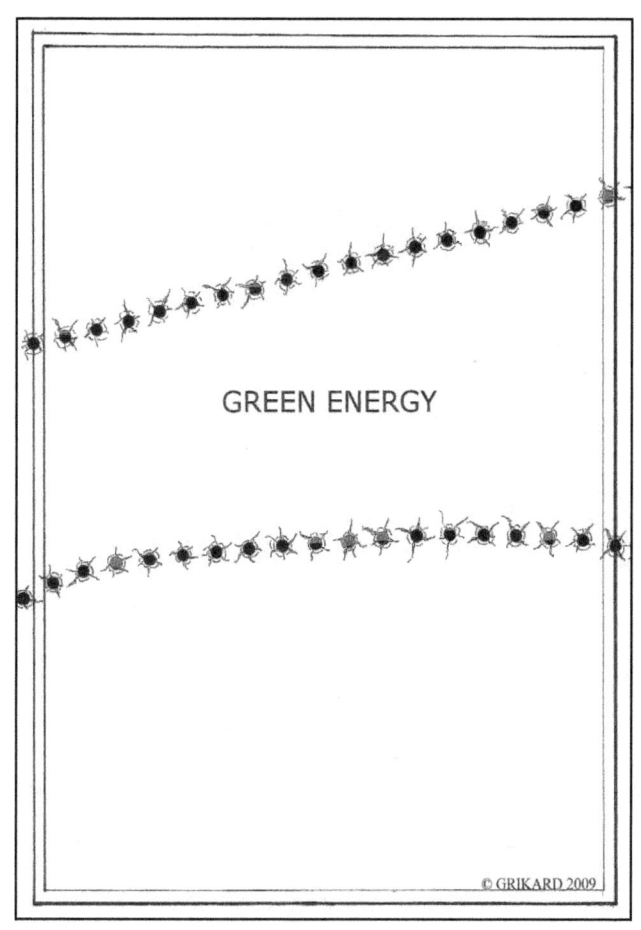

GREEN ENERGY

© GRIKARD 2009

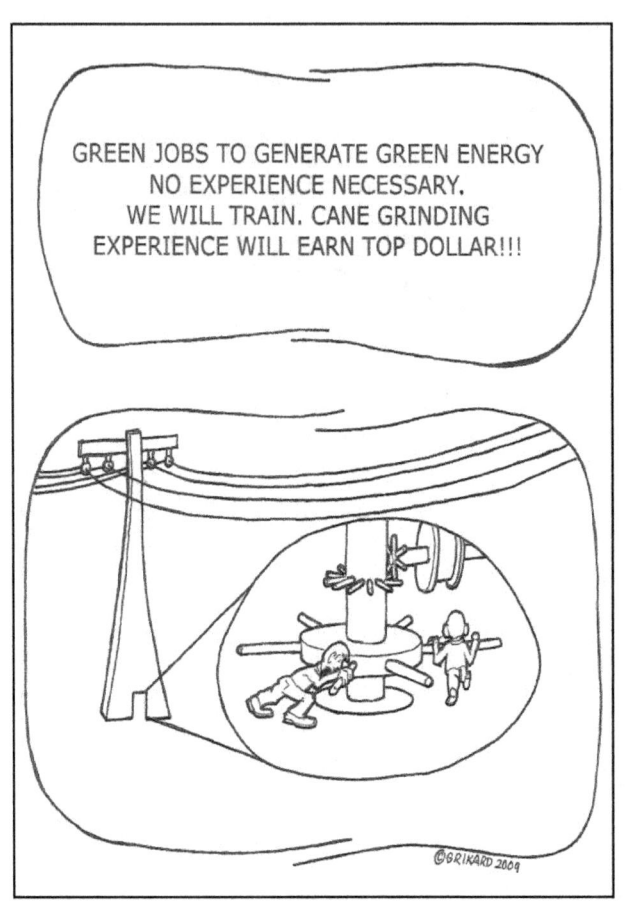

You **will** develop green energy.

Gas production process

Gas Production Process

Capturing and measuring methane gas has finally been solved. The theory of operation is as follows: gas produced by the animal is funneled through a hose that runs from the animal's rear to the gas meter. Gas is counted as it passes through the meter into the gas bladder.

New green jobs will be available for meter readers and gas bladder collectors. The meter readings will be needed for tracking and tax purposes.

The collected gas will be used in the new green car designed by Barney Franks which will be available in late 2010.

See Barney's design in the green car section.

Perpetual Green Energy System

Perpetual Green Energy System

This system would be deployed in areas of insufficient natural wind or areas isolated from the electrical grid.

The theory of operation begins with starting the gas generator by depressing the start button. The gas generator provides electrical power to the fan. When the fan reaches top speed the wind generator blades will be rotating one revolution per second causing the gas generator to stop. The fan will continue to operate because the wind generator provides electricity to the fan and the fan supplies the breeze to keep the wind generator turning which keeps the fan turning. The fan's breeze turns the blades of the wind generator which in turn operates the fan and the process repeats itself until the fan is turned off. This system sounds like something Obama's advisors would fund through earmarks.

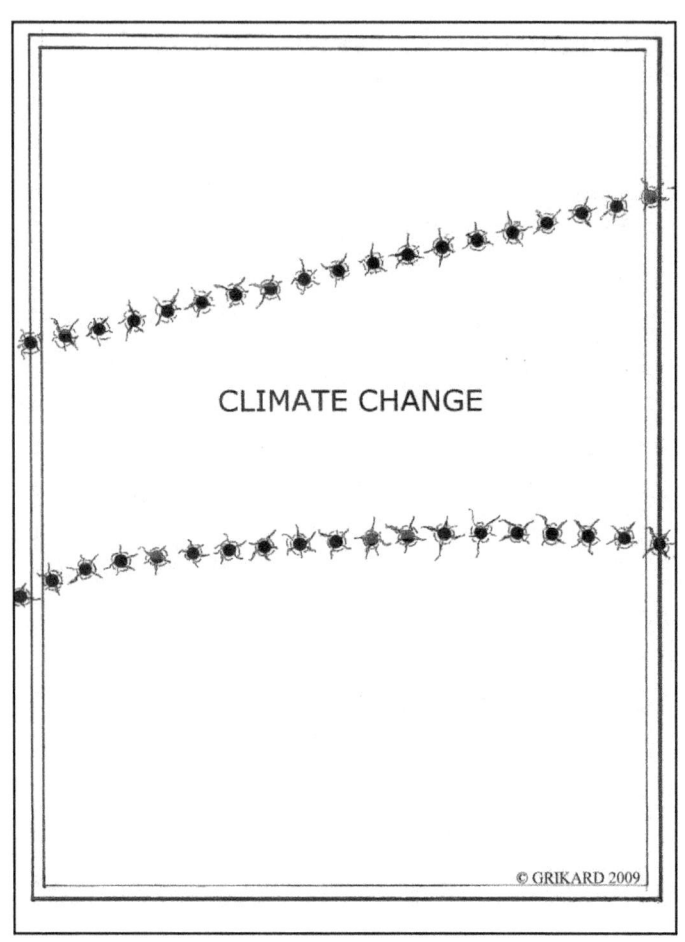

CLIMATE CHANGE

© GRIKARD 2009

Al Gore's climate change (global warming) theory only works if the earth is enclosed in a bubble...

...but, gravity pulls items to earth from space and lighter than air molecules escape from earth's atmosphere. Look, no bubble!

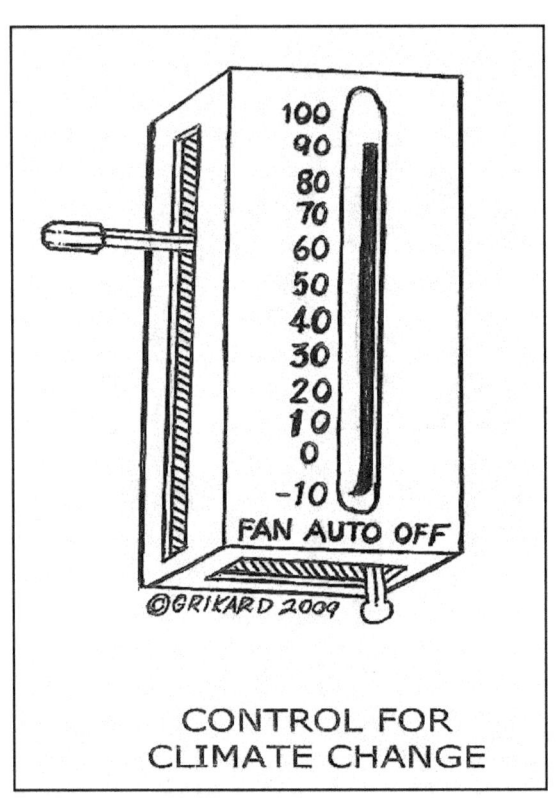

CONTROL FOR
CLIMATE CHANGE

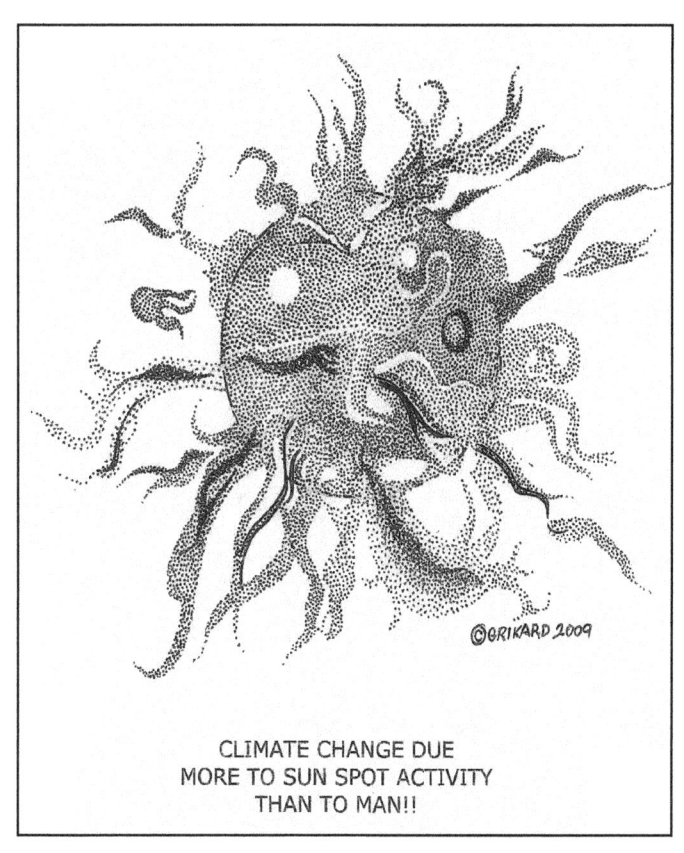

CLIMATE CHANGE DUE
MORE TO SUN SPOT ACTIVITY
THAN TO MAN!!

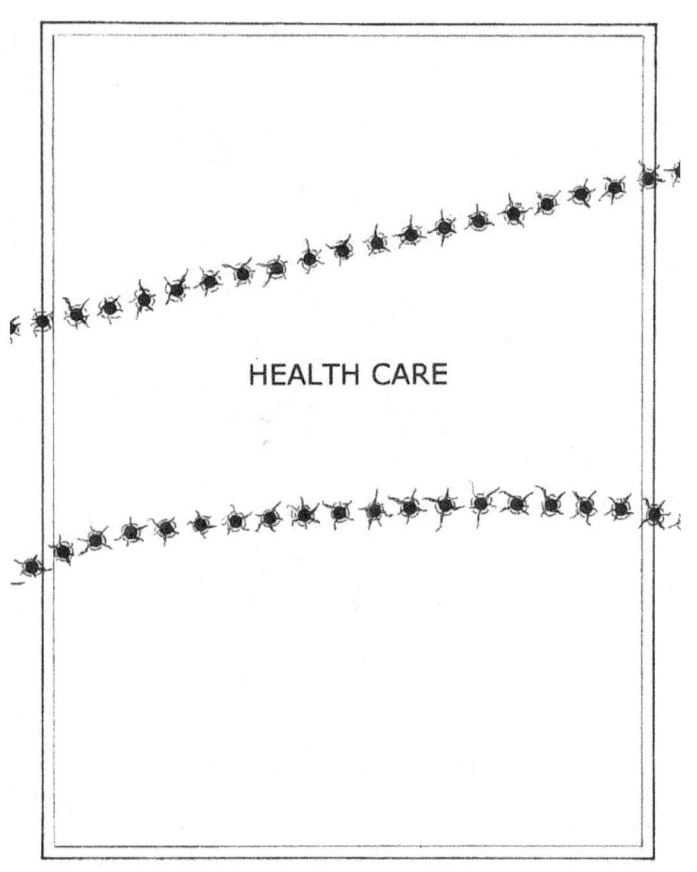

HEALTH CARE

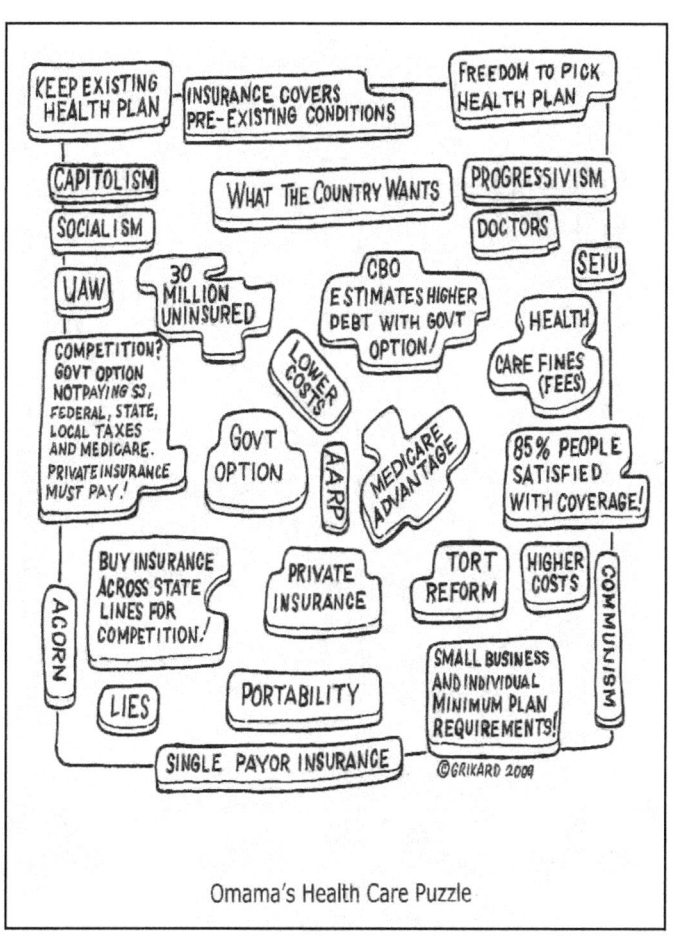

Omama's Health Care Puzzle

85

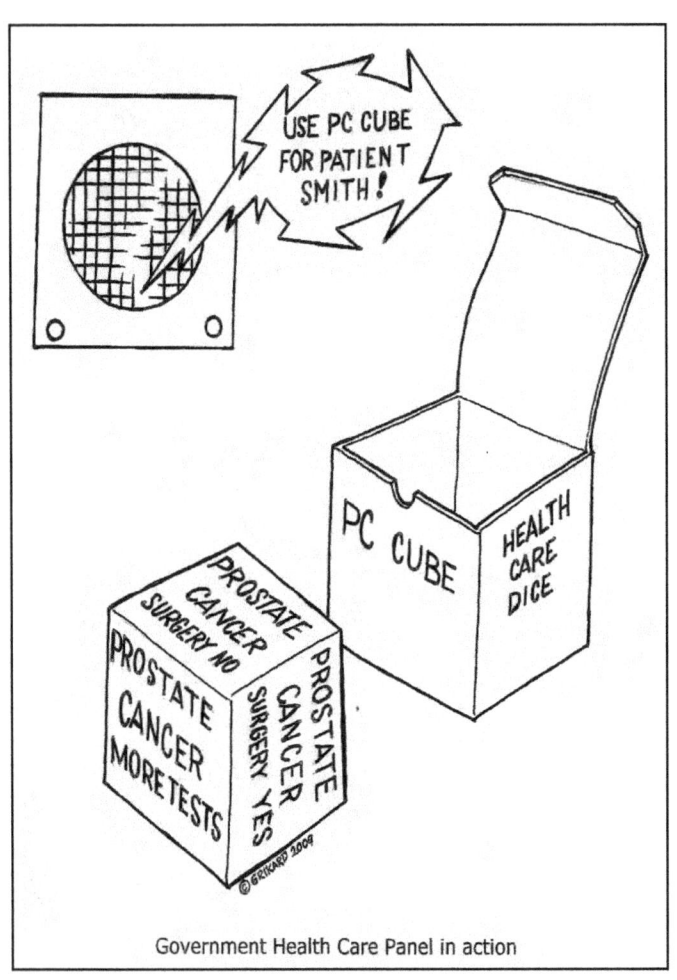

Government Health Care Panel in action

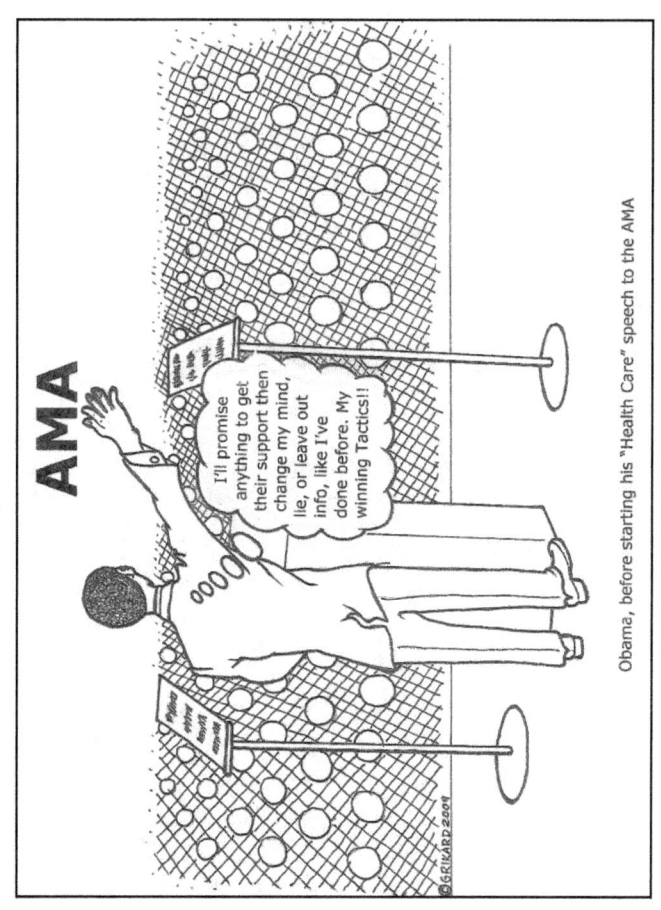

Obama, before starting his "Health Care" speech to the AMA

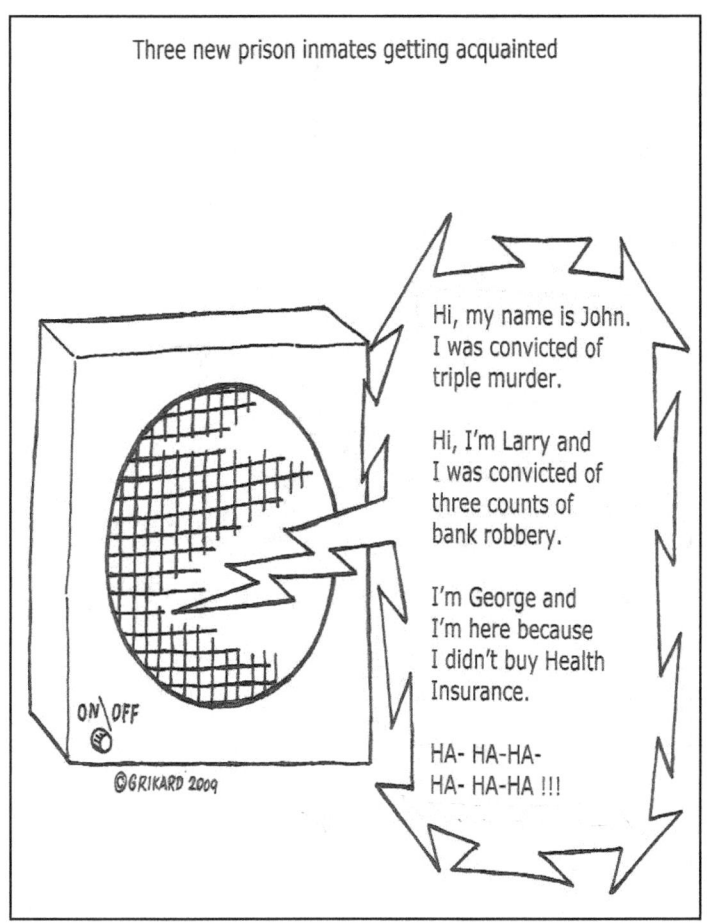

The Mexican Border

This is what I think will happen now that Obama's Health Care Bill has been signed into law. A flood of illegal immigrants will cross our borders to get free health care and who can blame them. Obama keeps saying illegal immigrants will not be eligible but his immigration reform will give the illegal's amnesty. Between now and when Obama's immigration reform passes, the border will be flooded. The liberals don't care about the immigrants they are only interested in their votes to keep the liberals in power. That's the way I see it. You may disagree, buts that's my opinion. What's yours?

93

Notes

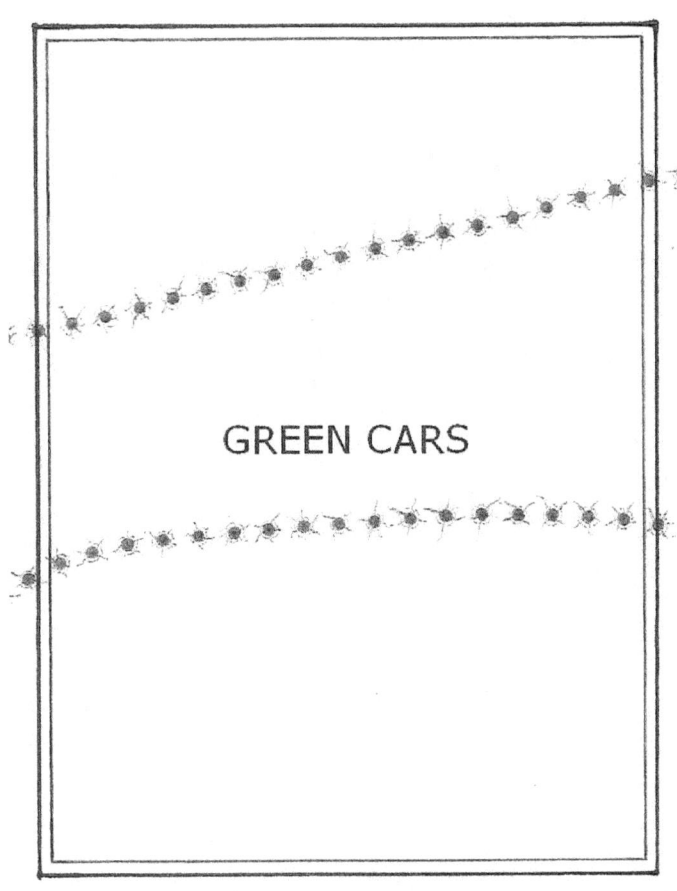

GREEN CARS

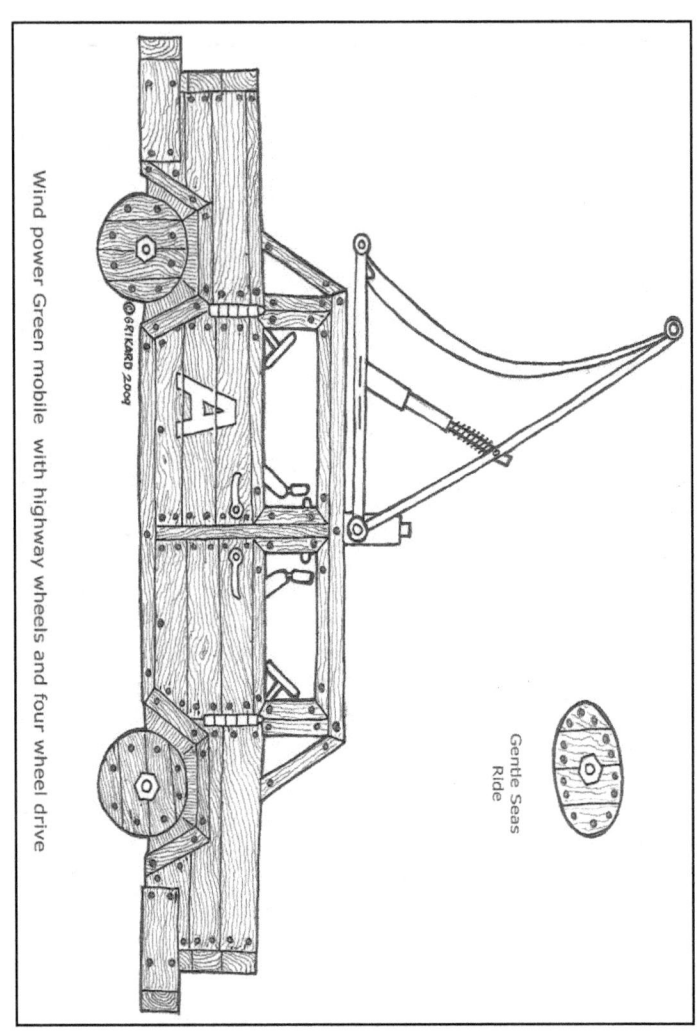

Wind power Green mobile with highway wheels and four wheel drive

Gentle Seas Ride

©6RIKARD 2009

96

Wind Powered Green Car

Here's an example of a green car. This one was designed by Nancy Pelosi. The main advantages are it's powered by the wind and made entirely of wood except for the superstructure which is aluminum tubing. The biggest disadvantage is the entire highway system will need to be widened to 200 ft for each two lane road. The cost will approach twenty trillion dollars. Nancy claims the car will create ten million jobs, five million to cut boards for production and repair, another five million to widen the highways.

As you can see from the first design drawings the car has a true four wheel drive system requiring two drivers for efficiency.

The only required preventive maintenance is resetting the nails on a monthly schedule.

I know everyone will want one. How about you?

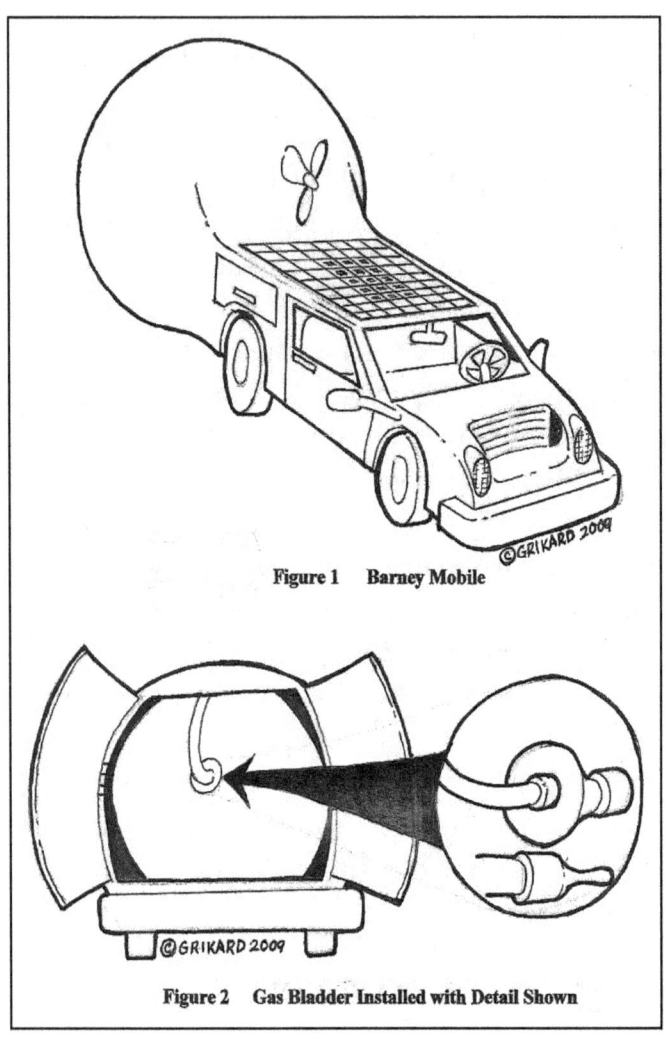

Figure 1   Barney Mobile

Figure 2   Gas Bladder Installed with Detail Shown

98

Barney Mobile

Here we have another green car. This one designed by Barney Franks. We know how his congressional committee influenced the housing market crash through his Fannie May/Freddie Mac oversight responsibilities.

Maybe Barney's design for an energy efficient green car that uses methane gas will be more successful. The methane gas production and collection process was covered earlier in the Green Energy section. The fuel captured in large rubber-like bags will be available soon after the auto goes into production.

With years, maybe months, maybe weeks, maybe days, maybe hours, maybe minutes, maybe seconds of business experience, Barney will propel his car to stardom.

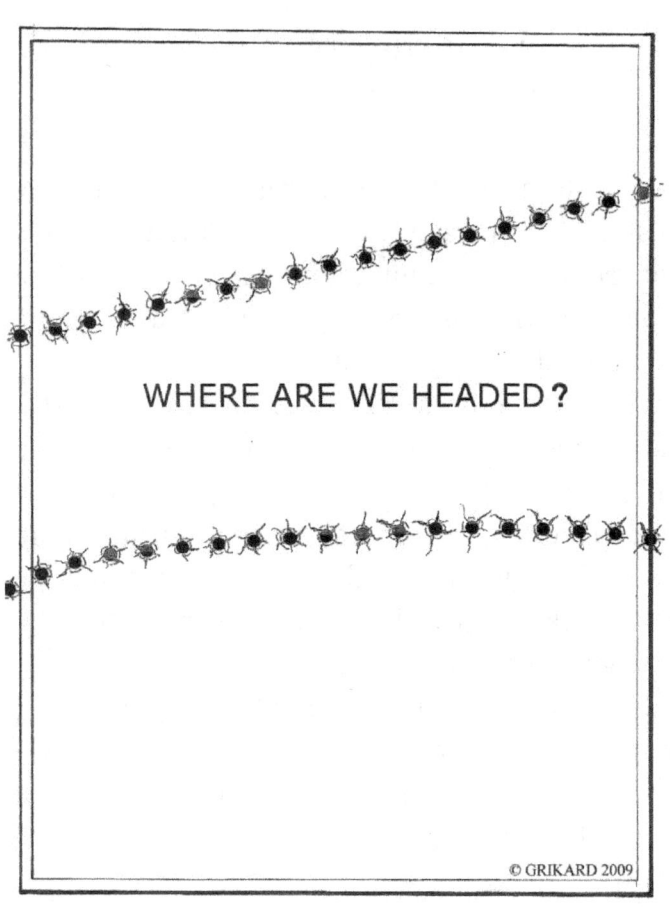

WHERE ARE WE HEADED?

© GRIKARD 2009

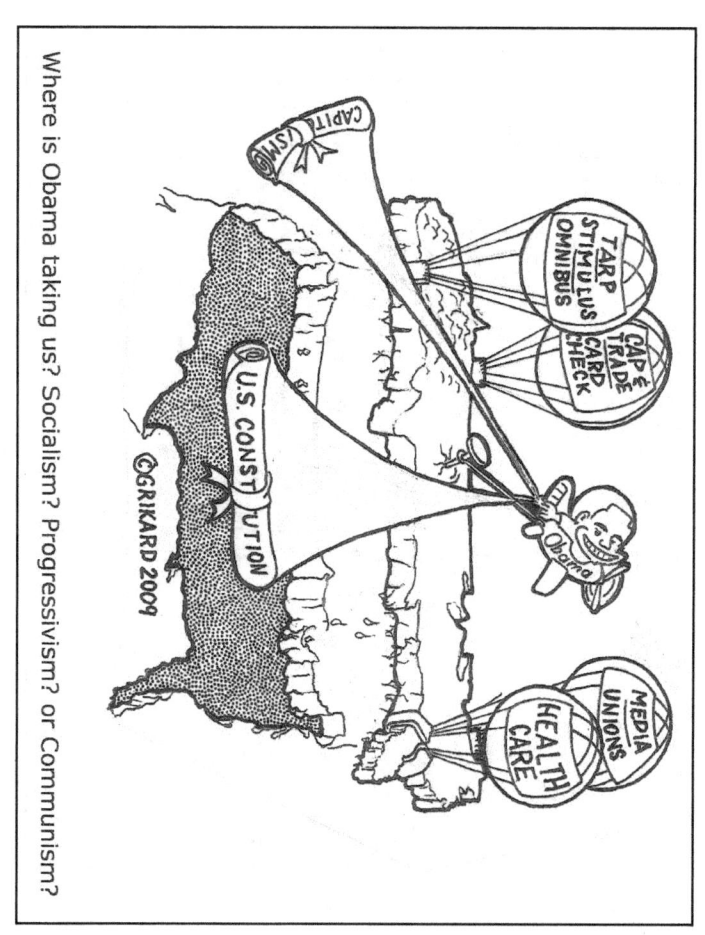

Where is Obama taking us? Socialism? Progressivism? or Communism?

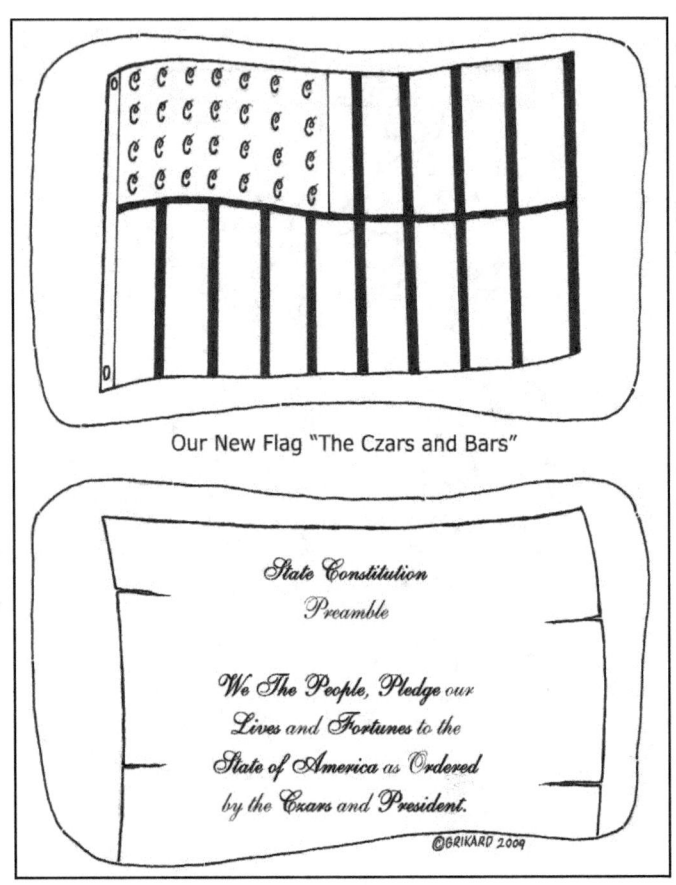

Our New Flag "The Czars and Bars"

State Constitution
Preamble

We The People, Pledge our Lives and Fortunes to the State of America as Ordered by the Czars and President.

©BRIKARD 2009

Czars and Bars

If the Obama administration is allowed to push all the progressive programs through Congress, we the American Nation will no longer be a Free Capitalist society.

Our flag will change from the Stars and Stripes to the Czars and Bars. Our individual rights granted in the Bill of Rights will only live in the history books.

The Constitution will change from The United States of America to the State of America, where we will be directed by the Czars and President.

Do I believe this will actually happen? No, but I believe it could happen.

Political Parties Need to Consider

All interested parties should have a national organization meeting. The purpose is not to select a presidential candidate, but to select the principles under which potential candidates are to be judged. This meeting is critical for the up-coming elections. We need to keep the two party political system because strength will be diluted if a third party is formed.

The Democrats have given the Republicans a platform to consolidate their base for the elections. The Democrats keep saying the "Republicans are the party of no." Why not use the word "no" to our advantage.

You can say no to Obama's programs, but you must have alternative answers.

Yes to spending of necessity, security and national defense.

Yes to line item veto.

Yes to small government.

Yes to health care improvements to existing system.

Yes to developing all types of energy.

Yes to states that want "right to work laws", not forced into organized labor.

Yes to constitutional politics, giving rights back to the states.

Yes to constitutional representatives.

I believe Congress should declare "war" on Al Qaeda and the Taliban. We must eliminate them where we find them. If the occupied country won't or can't kick the terrorists out, we will. Just stay out of our way. This one act will clarify our intensions to defeat the enemy. All nations that supply our enemies will be subject to blockades and/or legal action in national and world courts. U.S. companies that sell munitions to terrorists directly or indirectly will be fined or closed. The company leaders will be fined, imprisoned or both. All enemy combatants will be tried in military courts. Declaring war should put Iran and North Korea in their place. Without the war declaration we allow ourselves to be dragged into a long Viet Nam type engagement.

Once Obama is defeated in 2012, all federal agencies and levels of government that are not essential to security and the Defense Department should be temporally placed on 32 hour week schedules. Salaried employees pay will be cut 20%. Utilities and building upkeep will drop proportionally. The temporary status will remain in effect until the unemployment drops to 7%. State and local governments will be encouraged to follow the federal example. All levels of government should operate like our citizens are forced to. If you don't have the money, don't make the purchase.

I hope you'll consider one more suggestion. Social Security, Medicare, and Medicaid should be privatized. Social Security funds should be put in conservative index mutual funds. Since 1926, the stock market has made money during every ten year period. Compare that with congressional management of anything.

Obama's Poem

Obama's climb to power,
Starts with plans to devour,
Our national code of living,
That shrinks by the hour.

His plan conceals true course,
With rosy tales of perfection,
That confuse, disrupt and mislead,
Without experience or direction.

The rule is large with speed,
So opposition will not find,
To pass the bills unseen,
Keeps all unwilling behind.

With programs sent by deception,
That tax us now and forever,
Our children without future,
Means progress comes but never.

America's course is turning,
Obama's future is churning,
To remove him by vote,
Keeps our nation afloat.

Our Constitution is at stake,
We must unite to take
The country from bailouts and lies,
This promissory oath we must make.

Our economy is on the rise,
To reduce our national debt.
The Socialist programs of the past,
Will dissolve if Capitolism
Is allowed to last.

Our military keeps us safe,
Through wars that give and take,
To these we must not waver,
Who have suffered for our sake.
We must unite without fear,
To defeat our enemy is clear.

Our leaders must be wise,
To reverse our nation's plight,
The job is yours and mine,
To find Constitutional minds.

Notes

Notes

www.ingramcontent.com/pod-product-compliance
Lightning Source LLC
Chambersburg PA
CBHW072209280526
45788CB00002B/944